it's all about

TECHNIQUE

A Leisure Arts Publication by
Nancy M. Hill of

Acknowledgments

We have made every effort to ensure that these instruments are accurate and complete. We cannot, however, be responsible for human error, typographical mistakes, or variations in individual work.

It's All About Technique is the fourth in a series of books written by NanC and Company and published by Leisure Arts, Inc.

Author: Nancy M. Hill
Graphic Artist: Ty Thomson
Design Director: Candice Snyder
Assistant to Director: Candice Smoot
Cover Design: Maren Ogden &
Miriam DeRosier
Copy Editor: Dr. Sharon Staples

Front Cover: Corner – Tammy Mellish

For information about sales visit the Leisure Arts web site at www.leisurearts.com

Dear Scrapbooker,

This two-page spread of three of my granddaughters was made from a single photo. The girls and I had been shopping at the mall for a bit and as we were leaving I took their picture with my new digital camera. Their mother was complaining that they were not dressed for picture taking, they were anxious to go swimming and I only had time for one shot before the whining began. Fortunately, that one photo streeeetched a long way. Using a home photo printer, I printed 2 regular 4 x 6 photos, a distorted 4 x 6, and a blown-up and cropped photo of each of the girls. I chose Leisure Arts Memories in the Making paper and asked our designer, Camille Jensen, to do something creative with the photos. I am delighted with the finished two-page design and amazed at what can be done with one, very quick shot!

When we began this technique book I made a very neat working outline of all the possible scrapbooking and paper-crafting techniques I had used or observed. It was my intention to include them all in the 'table of contents' and showcase one or two designs featuring each technique. Boy, was I dreaming! It wasn't very long before I realized that there are far more techniques and creative possibilities than can be featured or described in a publication of this size. An encyclopedia may be more appropriate!

To narrow the scope of this project we chose a variety of techniques to focus on. From the simple to the complex and the trendy to the time-honored we have included detailed instructions for duplicating the techniques highlighted on the pages featured.

Happy Scrapping,

Nancy

Table of Contents

abrics, Textures & Weaves

People are likely to spend more time looking at a textured scrapbook page. The eye wanders back and forth between contrasting textures, and the hand is tempted to reach out and feel the page. Using contrasting textures adds dimension and interest. For example, a delicate or shiny, metal embellishment really stands out on a grainy, rustic fabric. Weaving is not only a nice embellishment, but also a great way to combine and layer textures on a page.

Madeline

Supplies - Patterned Vellum: Forget Me Not Designs; Vellum: Laura Ashley; Buckle: Making Memories; Cork: Magic Scraps; Metals: Making Memories; Conchos: Scrapworks; Date Stamp: Making Memories; Buttons: Doodlebug; Die Cut Flowers: Forget Me Not Designs; Beads: Magic Scraps

Construction Tips:
Use cork, paper or other textures in buckle clips instead of always using ribbon.

Designer: Crystal Pearson

1

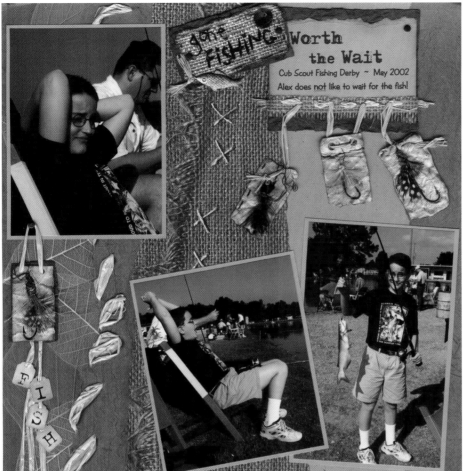

Gone FISHING... Worth the Wait

Cub Scout Fishing Derby ~ May 2002

Alex does not like to wait for the fish!

Worth The Wait

Supplies – Patterned Paper: NRN Designs; Die Cuts: NRN Designs; Stickers: NRN Designs; Ink: Stampin' Up; Embossing Powder: Stamps 'n' Stuff; Wire: Artistic Wire; Metallic Rub-ons: Craf-T; Brads: All The Extras

Construction Tips:

Distress fish tags by crumpling and inking tags. Embellish tags with fiber and wire and attach to page with raffia.

Construction Tips:

Fill vellum envelopes with tags that can be removed for a closer look.

Horsin' Around

Supplies – Patterned Paper: Paper Adventures, Leisure Arts, Creative Imaginations; Cardstock: Bazzill; Chalk: Craf-T; Eyelets: Making Memories; Silver Clip: Making Memories; Raffia: Making Memories; Buttons: Making Memories; Vellum Envelopes: Robin's Nest; Charm: The Card Collection; Font: CK Around

HORSIN around

NOT ONLY DO YOU HAVE PRINCESS SHOES ON BUT THEY ARE ON THE WRONG FEET (SEE LEFT, OOPS)

ONCE A PRINCESS, ALWAYS A PRINCESS, EVEN IN THE SADDLE!

Designer: Wanda E. Santiago

A Moment Of Wonder

Supplies — Stickers: Chatterbox,
Creative Imaginations; Pen: Krylon

Construction Tips:

Use pre-made stickers
to create a textured
background without
the bulk.

Designer: Laura Stewart

Grandpa's swing is loved by
all the Grandchildren that come
to visit. It even existed when I
was a little girl. We love you
Grandpa, forever and ever.
Zach and Jasmaine 03/31/2002

Family

Supplies — Patterned Paper: Chatterbox; Stickers: Anna Griffin; Eyelet: Making Memories; Embellishments: K & Co.; Mesh: Magic Mesh

Construction Tips:

Create a common message board with cardstock, buttons and ribbon. Pull the ribbon tight before adhering to the cardstock.

Designer: Debbie Campa

Grandpa's Swing

Supplies — Patterned Paper: Paper Adventures; Stamps: Provo Craft; Fonts: CK Script, Marisa, Sonja

Construction Tips:

To heat stamp vinyl:
1. Cut vinyl to 4 times the size of the image to be stamped.
2. Place vinyl on stamping mat and heat until vinyl begins to melt (heat vinyl evenly to ensure a uniform image).
3. Press stamp into vinyl; don't remove until vinyl cools (approximately 20 seconds).
4. Cut out vinyl to desired shape.

9

Embossing

Embossing adds a nice finishing touch to just about any page element imaginable. The most common forms of embossing are color and clear heat embossing and dry embossing. Clear embossing powder comes in two different forms: 1) regular powder which forms a thin, glass-like coating, and 2) deep powder which is applied in many layers to form a thick, clear coating. The thick coating can then be cracked for an aged look. Dry embossing can give a subtle elegance to a layout or a dramatic look with chalk. Use embossing powder with stamps and clay to add variety. Regardless of what type of embossing is used, the end result adds color, shine or dimension to a layout.

Designer: Janet Hopkins

smile

giggle

play

Enjoy the little things in life, for one day you may look around and realize they were the BIG things.

Smile, Play, Giggle

Supplies – Cardstock: Bazzill;
Acrylic Paints: Americana; Brads:
Boxer; Embossing Powder: Rubba
Dub Dub, Inc.; Metal Words:
Making Memories; Stamp Pad:
Versamark

Construction Tips:

Heat emboss torn edges by stamping area to be embossed, dusting with copper embossing powder (remove excess powder) and applying heat to the powder with an embossing gun.

Construction Tips:

Create stamped clay leaves by rolling clay to 1/8" thick, covering with metallic rub-ons and stamping with rubber stamps. Dust clay with embossing powder, spray with water and let dry.

Remember When

Supplies – Patterned Paper:
Chatterbox; Mulberry
Paper: Making Memories;
Cardstock: Bazzill,
Chatterbox; Rub-ons: Provo
Craft, What's New, Ltd.,
Craft Products, Inc.;
Stamps: Stampin' Up; Clay:
Provo Craft; Tags: Rusty
Pickle; Tiles: Sticko; Crystal
Effects: Stampin' Up

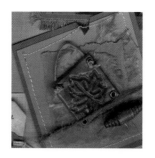

I Love My Family

...FALL

All the
reasons why
IT IS

fabulous

Designer: Sherri Allsman

Posing For Papa

Supplies – Patterned Paper: Leisure Arts; Metallic
Frames: DCWV; Embossing Powder: Suze Weinberg

Construction Tips:

Use thick embossing enamel on die cut frames to
create a metallic look. Apply several coats of enamel
until the desired thickness and look is achieved.
Allow each coat to dry before applying the next coat.

Forever Young

Supplies – Patterned Paper: Karen Foster Design, Misty Teal;
Transparency: 3M; Sand Dollar: Leave Memories; UTEE:
Suze Weinberg; Embossing Powder: Stamps 'n' Stuff, Mark
Enterprises; Re-inkers: Fresco, Stampa Rosa; Fonts: Bradley
Hand, Papyrus

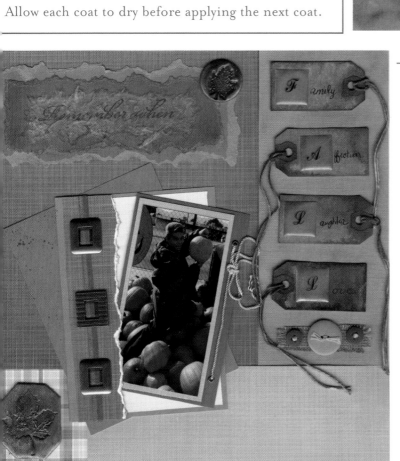

Construction Tips:

Create circle letters by
punching circles from
painted cardstock.
Deep emboss three lay-
ers with clear embossing
powder. Stamp letter
stamps into third clear
embossed layer while
still warm with gold ink.
Dip edges of circles into
gold embossing powder.

Curling, Tearing & Rolling

Curling, tearing and rolling paper are common techniques used to add variety to a layout, yet they are far from commonplace. There are endless ways to use these simple techniques to create extraordinary layouts. Try tearing paper to create designs, rolling paper back to reveal a beautiful photo or curling torn edges of paper for a subtle accent that adds the finishing touch to a layout.

Designer: Maegan Hall

Cherish

Supplies – Patterned Paper: Sonnets, Daisy D; Cardstock: Paper Garden; Metallic Word: Making Memories; Beads: Bead Heaven

Construction Tips:

Wet scrap paper with water, crumple and tear into various sized circles while still wet. Adhere flowers to layout, chalk edges with metallic rub-ons and finish by adhering beads to the center of each flower.

Hooray For Spring

Supplies – Patterned Paper: Deja Views; Black Pen: Creative Memories; Eyelets: Making Memories; Die Cut System: Sizzix; Twistel: Making Memories; Stickers: Jolee's By You; Glue: Tombo

Construction Tips:

Create rolled paper frame by:

1. Cutting out eight pieces of 4" x 5" paper.
2. Tightly roll the 5" edge of the paper around a pencil or rod.
3. Secure the entire seam of the roll with small pieces of tape.
4. Glue rolls to the photo and to each other (if you would prefer not to glue paper to your photo, mat the photo and glue rolls to the mat).

Hooray for Spring

There are so many things about Spring that we love. Even things we do throughout the year (like gardening, picnics or just playing with Derby) seem a little more special during Spring. It's definitely our favorite time of the year.

Spring 2001

Gardening

Picnics

Playing with

Derby

Designer: Leah Fung

friends

love

Don't walk in front of me...
I may not follow.
Don't walk behind me...
I may not lead.
Walk beside me...
And be my friend!
~Albert Camus

aspire

beauty

Friendship
the state of being friends

Designer: Sam Cousins

Walk Beside Me And Be My Friend

Supplies – Patterned Paper: NRN Designs, Paperbilities; Eyelets: Eyelets Every Month; Fiber: Fibers By The Yard; Definition: Making Memories; Rub-ons: Making Memories; Tags: Making Memories; Snaps: Making Memories; Font: P22 Type Foundry Monet

Construction Tips:

Tear a photo and ink the edges to give an aged look.

Designer: Leah Fung

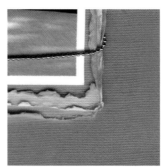

Construction Tips:

Curl torn paper by wetting the torn edges and curling by hand. When the paper dries the curls will remain.

I love and I am loved
more than I ever thought possible

Mothers Day
2003

More Than I Ever Thought Possible

Supplies – Cardstock: Bazzill; Beaded Chain: Making Memories; Eyelets: Making Memories

SPLISH SPLASH

Designer: Kim Heston

The West

Supplies – Patterned Paper: Leisure Arts, Design Originals; Eyelets: Making Memories; Hinge: Demis Products; Glue: Tombo

Construction Tips:

Tear strip of patterned paper, sand and roll edges. Adhere to page with a zig-zag stitch.

My dear Andrew,

I have always loved California, but I'm so happy knowing that you love it too. The beautiful weather, living on the coast, and being close to family is such a blessing. And, I love the fact that I can walk through our beautiful canyon all year round with you.

I love you.

Mom

AUG 0 5 2003

Designer: Leah Fung

James can't let Corey just sit and play peacefully! He tries to stir up trouble. He makes the first move by throwing wet sand at Corey and the fight begins. The older Corey gets he is able to give James a run for his money. Corey gets tired but is determined. The fight always seems to turn to me eventually.

Splish Splash

The torn cardstocks and mulberry papers work really well with the beach theme.

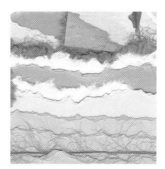

Construction Tips:

Tearing paper is easier when the paper is wet. Combine colored fibers and torn paper to give the layout a more finished look.

esh

Mesh is a versatile element in scrapbooking. It is easy to use and a great way to add texture to a layout. Mesh is often used to mat photos and journaling or as an embellishment to a layout. Mesh can also be used to create elements on your page such as a fishing or basketball net. Experiment with mesh on your next layout and experience for yourself its versatility.

Construction Tips:
Use safety pins to attach the mesh photo mats to one another.

Designer: Martha Crowther

Dream, Believe, Create And Inspire

Supplies — Patterned Paper: Paper Adventures; Fiber: Fibers By The Yard; Metal Accents: Li'l Davis Designs, Rebecca Sower Nostalgiques; Mesh: Magic Scraps; Font: Two Peas In A Bucket Jones Neighborhood

Today I Am Four

Supplies – Cardstock: Bazzill;
Mesh: Magic Mesh; Brads:
Embellish This; Font: Two Peas
In A Bucket Silly

Construction Tips:

Use mesh as a border to add
a lot of texture without bulk.

Designer: Jlyne Hanback

The Beauty Of Life

Supplies – Textured Paper: Artistic Scrapper; Cardstock:
Bazzill; Netting: Magic Scraps; Starfish: U.S. Shell, Inc.;
Embossing Powder: Ranger; Charm: Embellish It;
Metallic Rub-ons: Craf-T; Tag: Avery; Star: Provo Craft;
Stamps: PSX, Hero Arts; Stamp Pad: Excelsior

Construction Tips:

1. Cut mesh, distress by tearing
   some areas of the mesh and
   adhere to layout.
2. Create bronze portion of tag
   by crumpling beige cardstock, applying metallic rub-
   on and heat embossing with
   bronze embossing powder.

shabby Chic

Shabby chic is for all of you who like an antique feel with a fresh twist. It combines the old and new to form a contemporary feel. You can create a shabby chic look by antiquing and distressing your new photos and accents or by combining your old photos and accents with the new. No matter how you create your fresh, vintage look, enjoy the many possibilities of shabby chic.

Designer: Jama Wilson

Happy Hearts

Supplies – Stamps: PSX; Metallic Rub-ons: Craf-T; Nail Heads: Jewel Craft

Construction Tips:
1. Create distressed paper by crumpling and applying metallic rub-ons and ink to the paper.
2. Create 'hearts' portion of title by stamping letters onto tan cardstock, cutting out and adhering to layout. Adhere round page pebbles atop stamped letters.

Adventure Hat

Supplies – Patterned Paper: Club Scrap;
Cardstock: Club Scrap; Stamps: Stamp Craft, Club
Scrap; Cutouts: Rebecca Sower; Ink: Vivid!,
Making Memories, Versamark; Chalk: Craf-T

Construction Tips:

Create aged mat by wetting
and crumpling tan card-
stock. When the cardstock
is dry, flatten and chalk.

Construction Tips:

Repeat elements throughout
your layout, such as the mesh,
to pull the page together.

The Smoking Bride

Supplies – Patterned Paper: Paper
Illusions; Netting: Magic Scraps; Stickers:
K & Co., Rebecca Sower; Ribbon: Close
To My Heart; Frame: Anna Griffin Designs

Designer: Sherrill Ghilardi Pierre

14

focus

Focused scrapbook pages really tell a story about a child or event. The photos and journaling take you back to the very moment the page is documenting. Try adding focus to your pages by compiling similar photos onto one layout or by making the background simple to draw attention to the photos and journaling.

Experiencing life's little moments with you is experiencing them for the first time.

Designer: Gina Bergman

Life's Little Moments

Supplies - Patterned Paper: NRN Designs;
Cardstock: National Cardstock; Fiber: Ties
That Bind; Metal Clip: Making Memories;
Wax Seals: Sonnets; Chalk: EK Success;
Brads: Doodlebug; Font: BethsCute HMK

Construction Tips:

1. Match layout colors with the colors in the photo.
2. Adhere fibers to layout with mini glue dots.
3. Place large photos in a row across your layout to keep the focus on the photos.

Andrew, don't
move, I need to
wash your feet

How lucky am I to get a picture
of this? Alex, I've always known
that you loved your little
brother, but what a joy for me to
see you care for him in this way.
And, when you told Andrew to
stand still while you carefully
washed the dirt off his feet, it was
the first time that I really saw
your father in you.

Love you both very much,

Mom

Don't Move!

Supplies – Stickers: Rebecca Sowers
Nostalgique; Fonts: CK Gutenberg,
CK Typeset

Construction Tips:
Crop and enlarge photos
to emphasize the event
being described.

Please, Andrew

Pleeeease, Andrew

Supplies – Cardstock: Bazzill; Punch:
Marvy; Beaded Chain: Making Memories

Construction Tips:
Crop the photos to
show different parts of
the body and to add
focus to your subject.

Pleeeease, Andrew,
just one picture

My dear little Andrew,

Sometimes, I don't know why I
even try. It doesn't matter how
determined I am to take your
picture, you are MORE
determined to NOT take a
picture. It must look pretty silly
seeing a grown woman chase a
little boy around the front yard
with a camera, begging him to
take a picture. Well, one day,
I'm going to truly enjoy showing
these pictures to YOUR kids, and
I'll say "See this silly little boy?
That's your dad!"

I love you, Andrew.

Mom

Please, Andrew   Don't move   Please

Just one picture   No, no, don't move   Pleeease

Designer: Tammy Mellish

Diva In Shades

Supplies – Cardstock: Bazzill; Page
Pebbles: Making Memories

Construction Tips:

Use neutral colors for the
background. Enlarge and crop
photos in different shapes to
make the photos stand out.

Hot Summer Days

Supplies – Patterned Paper:
Wordsworth; Letters: Making
Memories, Simply Stated; Ink:
Close To My Heart

Construction Tips:

Choose a favorite
photo and create a
layout to enhance it.

Designer: Sherrill Ghilardi Pierre

18

ollage

Collage is often used in creating scrapbook pages. We were probably all given assignments in grade school to make a collage of some sort or another, but who knew how beautiful and fun they could be? Collages are not just a collection of magazine cutouts pasted onto a piece of cardboard; they are a collection of any items you wish. Many scrapbook backgrounds are created from a collage of different pieces of cardstock, paper and fabric. Try creating a collage of photos, paper or embellishments on your next scrapbook page.

Designer: Dawn McDowell

Construction Tips:

Crumple the bandana paper over and over again until it feels like fabric.

Ride Em, Partner

Supplies — Patterned Paper: Paperbilities; Cow Accent: Foofala; Rivet: Chatterbox; Ink: Ranger; Stamps: Hero Arts

Believe In Yourself

Supplies — Patterned Paper: Sarah Lugg, 7 Gypsies; Frame Charm: 7 Gypsies; Tag: Rusty Pickle; Skeleton Leaf: Lacey Paper Co.; Rub-ons: Making Memories; Frames: K & Co.; Label Holder: Making Memories; Clips and Rings: Making Memories; Bubble and Script Words: K & Co.; Clear Tag: K & Co.; Fiber Scraps: Bazzill; Glue Dots: Glue Dots International; Font: Microsoft Mistral

The World Is Before You

Supplies — Patterned Paper: Wordsworth,
Karen Foster; Cardstock: Bazzill; Ink: Close
to My Heart; Letters: Making Memories

Construction Tips:

When creating a collage use
memorabilia items such as a
copy of a birth certificate.

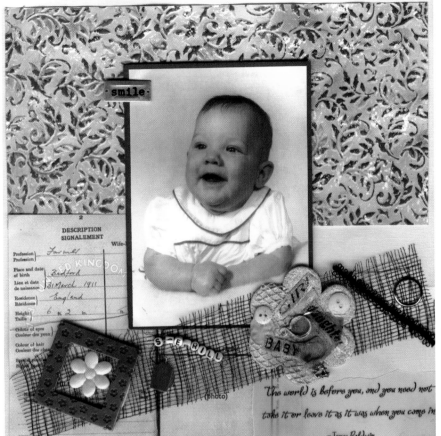

Designer: Sherrill Ghiardi Pierre

Designer: Sharon Laakkonen

Construction Tips:

1. Carry photo and strips of
   paper over centerline of two-
   page spread to make it look
   like one page.
2. Replace the fibers that come
   with the tag to colors that
   coordinate with the page.
3. Use metallic rub-ons for corners to give them a gold tone.

ixed Media

Create a mixed media look on your scrapbook pages by combining different arts and craft media. On your next layout try using stitching, stamping, inking, and embossing. It is fun to combine elements on a page that people do not expect to see together.

Designer: Ellen Bentley

Scrapbooking

Supplies – Patterned Paper: K & Co., Rocky Mountain Paper Co.; Stickers: NRN Designs; Letters: Foofala, Flavia, Sticko, Creative Imaginations; Quick Kutz: Mini Marissa; Stamps: Hero Arts

Flower Girls

Supplies – Patterned Paper: Bo Bunny, Paper Adventures, The Paper Company; Cardstock: National Cardstock; Tags: Making Memories; Floss: DMC; Flowers: Jolee's By You, My Mind's Eye; Page Pebbles: Making Memories; Eyelets: Making Memories

Look At This Face

Supplies – Patterned Paper: Terri Martin, Creative Imaginations; Transparency: HP; Buttons: Making Memories; Buttons: Making Memories; Bamboo Clips: All The Extras; Tag: KI Memories; Metal Heart: Making Memories; Pink Heart: Foofala; Font: Good Dog Plain

Construction Tips:

Choosing paper that expresses your theme is a great way to save time.

Look at this Face

Sometimes I wonder what goes through a four year olds brain. I bet it is "what am I going to play next, Power Rangers or Spiderman or Hulk" or "I want to run, hide, no I want to eat, no I want to roller blade or swim" May you always have simple and happy thoughts.

october 2, 2003

dream ♥ believe

Designer: Martha Crowther

Construction Tips:

Sew frames and borders with a decorative sewing machine stitch to add a home made feel to a layout.

Designer: Dezda Wengler

Black &White

Who doesn't love black and white? The simplicity, clean lines and contrast are appealing to so many of us. Black and white photos are not difficult to take and the end result is great. A tip for beginning photographers: keep the backgrounds simple and crop in close to the subject. Black and white is always classy and always in style.

Designer: Sheila Riddle

"Know how much I love you mommy?

As big as the sky and more den anyfing

Dat's how much I love you"

As told by Baylee, 3 ½ , Spring 2002

Construction Tips:
Attach black eyelets to torn vellum and thread with wire before adhering to the photo mat.

More 'Den Anyfing'

Supplies – Charm: Making Memories; Font: CK

Paparazzi

Supplies – Cardstock: Bazzill; Floss: DMC; Eyelets: Making Memories; Clothespin: Ellsworth Hall; Stamp: 2000 Plus

Construction Tips:

1. Hang the photos and subtitle to give the layout a darkroom feel.
2. Place three photos in a strip with eyelets to look like a film negative.

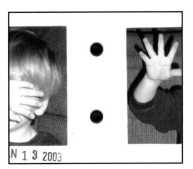

Photo Shoot

Supplies – Patterned Paper: Rusty Pickles; Transparency: HP; Fonts: Two Peas In A Bucket Blissful, Stamp Act

Construction Tips:

Place more photos on a layout by dividing a page into equal sections. Each section can be used for journaling, photos or an embellishment.

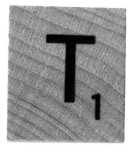

Titles

Titles say so much. They can be long or portray the theme of a page in one word. Take the time to think about what to title your page. They don't need to be cute or elegant, just exactly what you want.

Construction Tips:

Create a title strip that runs across the top, bottom or side of a layout. Use jump rings to attach punches that match the theme.

What Froggy Doing

Supplies — Patterned Paper: Magenta, Bo Bunny; Bookplate: Making Memories; Punch: Marvy; Jump Rings: Making Memories; Brads: Making Memories; Floss: DMC; Font: Times New Roman, Two Peas In A Bucket Falling Leaves

Construction Tips:

Scan large photo and use a software program to duplicate and change the color of the photo.

Original

Supplies — Patterned Paper: Rusty Pickles; Eyelets: Making Memories; Computer Program: Scrapbook Factory; Adhesive: Xyron; Glue: Tombo; Font: CK Typewriter

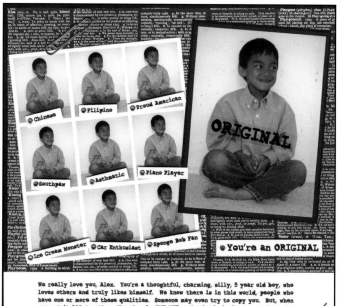

Home Is Where The Army Sends You

Supplies – Patterned Paper: Leisure Arts; Eyelet Letters: Making Memories; Alphabet Beads: Making Memories; Scrabble Tiles: Making Memories; Stickers: David Walker; Punches: Creative Memories, EK Success

Construction Tips:

Create titles using a variety of letter media. Combining the different media will give an interesting look to a page.

Designer: Miranda Isenberg

Designer: Sam Cousins

7 Wonders Of The World

Supplies – Border Stickers: Club Scraps; Fiber: All The Extras; Charm: All The Extras; Letter Stickers: David Walker, Sonnetts, Treehouse Design, Making Memories, Rebecca Sowers Nostalgique; Poemstone: Sonnets

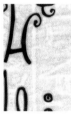

Construction Tips:

1. Create crayon rubbing by placing white paper over a piece of embossed hieroglyphic cardstock and rubbing with a crayon.
2. The title is from a story where a teacher asks children to list the seven wonders of the world. One girl's response was: touch, love, laugh, taste, see, hear, and feel.

nderstated Color

Understated color gives an easy, restful feel to a layout. They are easy to look at and a nice break from busier, more colorful pages. Monochromatic pages are often understated and reflective of the moment they are documenting. Mix things up in your scrapbook by adding some understated color pages. You will be pleased with the results.

Construction Tips:
Use an oversized frame to give a small photo substance.

Forever Friends

Supplies – Cardstock: Bazzill; Frame: This & That; Metals: Making Memories

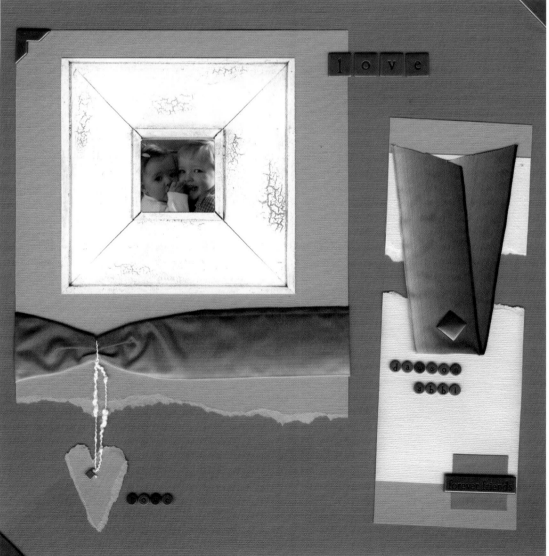

Designer: Jodi Sanford

His Laugh Is Contagious

Supplies – Cardstock: Bazzill; Punches: Paper Shapers; Stamps: Making Memories; Pencils: Primsicolor; Metal Frame: Making Memories; Fonts: Kayleigh, Times New Roman

JOSEPH DAVID

LOVING   SPIRITED   HAPPY   ADORABLE   CAREFREE

...five words to describe Joseph. His laugh is contagious, his hugs are irreplaceable and his smiles are unforgettable.

APR 2003

Designer: Tracy A. Weinzapfel Burgos

Construction Tips:
Create a different look by placing photos at the edge of your layout without mats.

Construction Tips:
A great layout can be made with nothing more than paper and vellum.

Sometimes

Supplies – Cardstock: Making Memories; Tinted Pens: Spot Pens

SOMETIMES...
Let's just blow bubbles,
For no good reason
Let's just blow bubbles
Laugh a little, watch them disappear
Not even wonder where.
Smile and touch the rainbow colors
Watch them float in the air.
No reason why–
No goals, no structure.

SOMETIMES...
Let's just
Blow bubbles

Unknown

Kelly Mieko Nakandakari

Summer 2000

28

ranslucent

So many different looks can be created with translucent paper. Vellum comes in different colors and patterns and transparencies are available, too. Use vellum to create the look of water or to make the background of a photo fade away. Translucent mediums are great for titles and journaling as well.

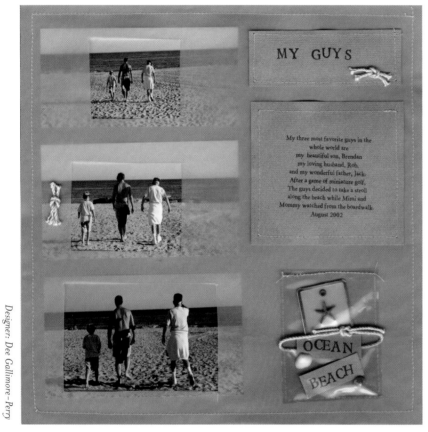

MY GUYS

My three most favorite guys in the whole world are my beautiful son, Brendan my loving husband, Rob, and my wonderful father, Jack. After a game of miniature golf, The guys decided to take a stroll along the beach while Mimi and Mommy watched from the boardwalk. August 2002

OCEAN BEACH

Designer: Dee Gallimore–Perry

My Guys

Supplies – Stamps: PSX; Shells: U.S. Shell, Inc.; Metal-Rimmed Tag: Making Memories; Glue Dots: Glue Dots International; Font: P22 Type Foundry Garamouche

Construction Tips:

Cut out holes in the vellum for the subject of the photos to show through. Stitch the vellum to the background.

Bucking Bronco

Supplies – Patterned Paper: Leisure Arts; Cardstock: DCWV; Vellum: DCWV; Rubons: Craf-T Products, Inc.; Frames: Leisure Arts; Leather: Dritz

Construction Tips:

Scan a photo into a software program and print onto a sheet of vellum. Tear the edges and mat with tan cardstock.

Our Buckaroo

The world is but a canvas to the Imagination

Designer: Camille Jensen

Snow in the Park

Kassidy

DEC 02 2002

No time like

Snow time

Snow In The Park

Supplies – Patterned Paper: Leisure
Arts; Vellum: Leisure Arts;
Snowflake Brads: Making Memories;
Charms: Leisure Arts; Stickers:
Leisure Arts; Font: CK Elusive

Construction Tips:
Attach torn vellum to
the bottom of a layout
to mimic snow.

Carpenteria Beach

Supplies – Cardstock: Bazzill; Picture Pebble:
Two Peas In A Bucket; Sea Shells: Magic
Scraps

Construction Tips:
Cut vellum into rectangles, fold
and punch holes to thread jute
through. Cut out corkboard
title with a template and place
into vellum pockets with sea glass
and a sand dollar.

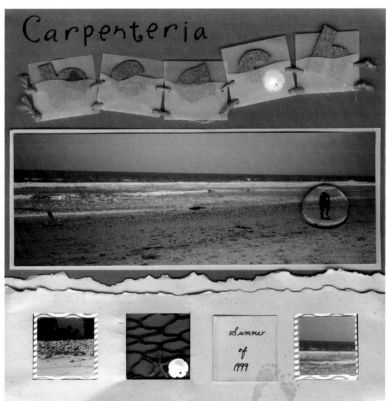

Carpenteria

Summer
of
1999

Designer: Gabrielle Mader

# hoto Manipulation

Manipulating photos is a favorite way to add variety to scrapbook pages. Image transfers, hand tinting, laminating, embossing, cropping and cutting are just a few ways to enhance your photos. This technique produces a lot of impact for your effort, so try new things and see how you can enhance your photos.

Construction Tips:
Use a photo manipulation program to print photos in different forms (artistic, brush strokes, stylized, etc.).

Construction Tips:
Enlarge a photo and crop different sections of the photo. Mat each section and then reassemble the photo.

Girl's Day Out

Supplies – Patterned Paper: Leisure Arts; Cardstock: DCWV; Vellum: DCWV, Leisure Arts; Stickers: Leisure Arts; Brads: Making Memories

I can only take so much traveling
And then I *have got* to have a day with my girls!
There is nothing *better* than grandkids–
And those three are a real treat!

We played, ate ice cream, went shopping
And, of course, took pictures!

Designer: Camille Jensen

37

Pick Of The Patch

Supplies — Patterned Paper: Leisure Arts; Cardstock: DCWV; Leaves: Family Treasures; Square Punches: Family Treasures; Stamps: Hero Arts, Simply Stamps; Beads: Provo Craft; Embossing Powder: Suze Weinberg; Concho: Scrapworks

Construction Tips:

Punch out squares of a double print. Adhere over the same spot on the original photo with pop dots.

Designer: Camille Jensen

Designer: Martha Crowther

Children look at the world with their perfect little hearts
Children are gifts to be treasured, which need to be shown love, patience, and fairness, that their value is known. They need freedom to grow, but with a strong guiding hand, to learn honesty, courage, and when to take a stand. Encouragement and praise should be directed their way, so dreams can be reached and goals accomplished each day. September 12, 2003

Children Are Gifts To Be Treasured

Supplies – Patterned Paper: Terri Martin, Creative Imaginations; Transparency: HP; Metal Trinkets: Lil' Davis Designs; Font: Bottled Fart

Construction Tips:

Give the impression of a larger photo by cutting the edge of a photo into strips. Keep the strips in order and reassemble the photo leaving space between each strip.

The Wild Child

Construction Tips:

Hand tint a black and white photo to add as much color as you like.

Designer: Vickie McMillan

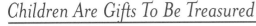

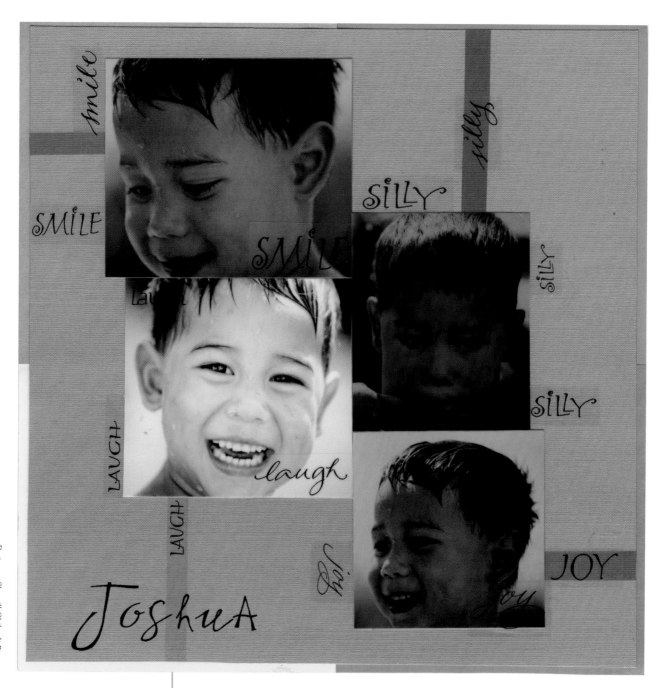

Designer: Sherrill Ghilardi Pierre

Silly, Silly Joshua

Supplies - Cardstock: Bazzill;
Stickers: Bo Bunny; Title: Making
Memories; Laminate Sheets: Xyron

Construction Tips:
Apply colored laminate
sheets to photos with a
Xyron Machine.

Mud

Supplies – Title: Wordsworth; Fiber:
Fibers By The Yard

Construction Tips:

Create a title background
from scrap pieces of
photos cut into strips.

The spring mud combined with an odd assortment of clothes to produce this little urchin girl in our backyard. Jaimee was excited to dress herself and venture into the warmer weather. 3/03

Designer: Jane Swanson

Designer: Ashley Smith

Nana's Girls

Supplies – Patterned Paper: Leisure
Arts, Made To Match; Mesh: Scrapbook
Diva; Font: CK Hustle

Construction Tips:

Adhere ribbon to the
edges of the cropped
photo and as a border
for the layout.

Color

Nothing can grab your attention quite like color. Using lots of color is fitting for joyous occasions, holidays and celebrations. Can you think of a better way to communicate a child's joyful personality on a scrapbook page than color? Don't be afraid to be bold and use the colors you love.

Designer: Janna Wilson

Construction Tips:
Bring a page together by choosing colors for a layout from the colors in the photos.

Sip Of Summer
Supplies – Patterned Paper: Leaving Prints, All About Me Co.; Vellum: The Paper Company; Metal Charms: Making Memories; Brads: Making Memories; Title: Creative Imaginations; Photo Corners: K & Co.; Font: CK Summer

All Girl

Supplies — Patterned Paper: Bazzill; Cardstock:
National Cardstock; Gingham: This & That;
Buttons: This & That; Eyelets: Doodlebug;
Beads: Bead

Construction Tips:

Cover enlarged photo with clear contact paper, dip it
in water and gently rub paper off the back of the
photo. The resulting image should be transparent.
Lightly sand the edges and adhere to the background.

Daphne, Pigtails And Cade

Supplies — Patterned Paper: Leisure Arts; Label
Holder: Making Memories; Font: CK Curly

Construction Tips:

Triple matting photos with
different colors is a great
way to add color to a layout.

Journaling

Journaling is used on almost every scrapbook page. It says what the photos cannot, like your feelings when you took the photo, the details of special events or even the date. Having children write their own journaling is a fun idea. They will be able to look back at the pages and be amazed at how their handwriting and spelling abilities have changed over the years. Hide journaling behind a tag or in a booklet if you would like to write your thoughts but don't want to share them with every person who looks at your scrapbook. You will be glad you took the time to add journaling to your page as your loved ones cherish what you have written, now and in the future.

Here come Abby's lips! And isn't this her color?! We didn't have to worry about it smudging off everywhere because she was so smart and used the "stay on" formula! These moments are priceless!
-June 2003-

Construction Tips:

Handwrite title onto cardstock with black chalk pencil. Blend colors together with a brush pen and then go over letters with a medium fine black pen.

Here come Abby's lips
isn't this her color?!
didn't have to worry
it smudging off ever
because she was so smar
used the "stay on" for
These moments are pr

Designer: Janna Wilson

Pucker Up

Supplies – Cardstock: Bazzill, DMD; Vellum: Treehouse Designs, Inc.; Pens: Zig, Sakura; Nail Heads: Jewel Craft; Fibers: Adornments; Tag: Making Memories; Ink: Crafters

Designer: Ashley Smith

Rock Star

Supplies – Patterned Paper: Leisure Arts;
Tags: Leisure Arts; Font: CK Child's Play

Construction Tips:
Create pockets behind photos to hide journaling.

Merry And Bright

Supplies – Patterned Paper: Leisure Arts;
Frames: Leisure Arts; Rub-on: Making
Memories; Clips: Making Memories; Labels:
Me & My Big Ideas; Font: CK Curly

Construction Tips:
Select a few images that capture the event you are scrapbooking, then describe the event in detail with the journaling.

Jesse (6) and Kassidy (1 1/2) had a wonderful Christmas 2002. These pictures are from Christmas morning at Nana's house. Kassidy absolutely loved opening the presents. He didn't care about what was inside them, he just liked the wrapping paper. Jesse, on the other hand, loved the presents. He got toys, games, CDs, and more toys! The boys, Dad, and I spent the whole morning playing at Nana's and then we went down the street to Grandma's house for Christmas dinner.

Designer: Ashley Smith

40

Designer: Leah Fung

Alex, you almost always want me to say our prayers. But, every now and then, you're willing to, and it makes me so happy. I just love hearing you thank God for things that are important to you. You really put a lot of thought into it. I want you to know that I thank God... for you.

I love you, Alex.

Mom

THANKS

I Thank God For You Too

Supplies – Patterned Paper: K & Co.; Eyelets: Making Memories; Font: Times New Roman

Construction Tips:

Create journaling by matting child's handwritten paper to the bottom half of a folded piece of black cardstock. Adhere the photo to the top of the other half of the black cardstock, so the photo will lift to reveal the journaling underneath.

Designer: Renee Villalobos–Campa

Family Time Together

Supplies – Patterned Paper: Scrap Ease; Cardstock: Bazzill; Eyelets: Making Memories; Floss: DMC; Die Cut System: Sizzix Fun Serif; Font: Little Trouble Girl

Construction Tips:

Create booklets by folding cardstock in half. Give the look of hinges with eyelets.

Dad took the day off from work so we could go to the Madison Zoo with Cook, Melissa, & Jena. It was such a hot day we had to keep splashing water on you to keep you cool. Except for your bright red cheeks, the heat hardly bothered you kids.

Michael loved feeding the goats pellets from an ice cream cone. The 1st time he tried it, the goat was too quick and ate the entire cone, pellets and all. Michael was so broken hearted; we had to let him buy another cone of pellets. That time he was prepared. Michael was crazy about the wild chipmunks. He crumbled up graham crackers on the ground and watched as they eagerly scurried to the crumbly feast.

Hunter was just happy to be out and about. He was wide-eyed; taking in all of the new sights and sounds.

My favorite thing about the day was the day itself. Spending family time together, with my 3 men, means everything to me.

Designer: Anna Estrada Davison

Today, My Sweet Child

Supplies – Patterned Paper: 7 Gypsies; Stickers: Sonnets; Buckle
Charm: Making Memories; Concho: 7 Gypsies; Folding Tag: Paper
Impressions; Ink Pad: Colorbok; Label Maker: Dymo

Construction Tips:

1. Have child press hand into chalk inkpad and then onto cardstock to create handprint.
2. Use the index print from the developer to make a nice, little group of photos.

Like A Rock

Supplies – Patterned Paper: Made
To Match; Tag: Paper Loft; Fiber:
Fibers By The Yard; Rub-on:
Making Memories; Metal Word:
Li'l Davis Designs

Construction Tips:

Print journaling onto vellum, tear the edges and apply chalk.

Joyful Journey

Supplies – Patterned Paper: Colorbok; Cardstock: Bazzill; Stamp: Close To My Heart; Charm: 7 Gypsies; Stickers: Rebecca Sower Nostalgiques

Construction Tips:

Cut out rectangles of corrugated cardboard and fold with a portion of black mat over photo. Staple cardboard and mat into place.

Dance, Cry, Sing

Supplies – Patterned Paper: Design Originals, Rusty Pickle; Stickers: Sonnets; Photo Corners: Canson; Chain: Making Memories; Heart Clip: Making Memories; Metal Words: Making Memories; Buttons: Dress It Up; Stamps: Hero Arts; Ric-Rac: Memory Lane Paper Co.; Ribbon: May Arts; Fibers: Rubba Dub Dub, Inc., Art Sanctum; Fonts: Two Peas In A Bucket Chestnuts, Straight-up, Microsoft Reference Serif

Construction Tips:

Creating a page of journaling is a great way to preserve your thoughts for future generations.

 # etals

Metals add texture, shine and interest to a page. So many metal embellishments are available to the scrapbooker: metal rimmed tags, brads, eyelets, letters, frames, etc. Embellish your next layout with metal; you will be amazed at how it can transform a page.

Home Is Where The Heart Is

Supplies – Patterned Paper: K & Co., Karen Foster, Daisy D's; Cardstock: Bazzill; Wire: Making Memories; Buttons: Making Memories; Date Stamp: Making Memories; Font: Two Peas In A Bucket Recital

Construction Tips:

1. Create script paper by typing Samuel Woodworth quote repeatedly and printing onto paper.
2. Attach hinges to paper with gold wire.

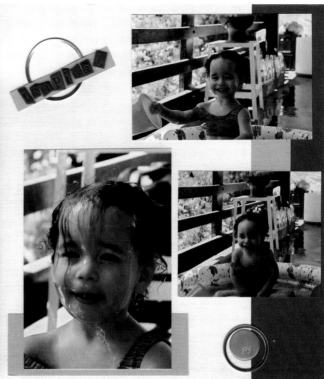

Beating The Heat

Supplies – Cardstock: Bazzill; Vellum: Paper Reflections; Metal Letters: Making Memories; Circle Tags: Making Memories; Poemstones: Sonnets

Construction Tips:

Soak metal tags in water for a short time to remove the paper centers easily.

The Most Beautiful Wedding

The Most Beautiful Wedding

Supplies – Fiber: Fibers By The Yard; Font: Two Peas In A Bucket Ringlet

Construction Tips:

Weave wire through the alphabet letters in addition to the floss to keep the letters in place.

# Tying It All Together

We love to use fiber and threads in our scrapbook pages to tie everything together. Not only are fibers and threads a great finishing touch to a layout, but they also add texture and color to a page. Use any fiber you can think of from fishing line to raffia to leather to yarn.

It's A Tie Game

Supplies – Patterned Paper: Leisure Arts; Cardstock: DCWV; Walnut Ink: 7 Gypsies; Stamps: Hero Arts; Mesh: Magenta; Fibers: DMC; Crackle Paint: Folk Art; Acrylic Paint: Delta; Baseball Snap: 7 Gypsies

Construction Tips:
Crackle paint frame and ink when dried.

Designer: Martha Crowther

Partners In Grime

Supplies – Transparencies: Clearly Creative; Circle Clips: Making Memories; Fiber: Fibers By The Yard; Fonts: Two Peas In A Bucket Brownies, Two Peas In A Bucket Chatter

Construction Tips:
Use fiber to outline photo and title words.

Designer: Valerie Barton

Little Cowboy

Supplies – Patterned Paper: Paper Loft, Club Scrap; Corrugated Cardboard: Paper Reflections; Star Brads: Magic Scraps; Transparency: Pockets On A Roll; Netting: Magic Scraps; Font: Stagecoach

Construction Tips:
Make a color copy of a toy gun and belt to use in the collage layout.

We spent Mother's Day weekend on Long Beach Island. The weather was gorgeous and we stayed at The Engleside Inn in Beach Haven. They had recently redone the rooms, so they were extra nice. We went on the beach, ate at Uncle Will's for breakfast, and took a ride up to Barnegat Lighthouse. It was windy, but warm with sunny, blue skies. Julia was obsessed with picking up tons of little rocks and since Grace was only 9 months old, she was content to hang out in her stroller. But she did try to crawl away from us on the beach! Julia even got to swim in the pool at the hotel which made her very happy. It was a really nice weekend! May 2001

Weekend At The Beach

Supplies – Patterned Vellum: EK Success;
Fiber: Brown Bag Fibers; Metal Snaps: Making
Memories; Paper Crimper: Fiskars; Font:
Creating Keepsakes

Construction Tips:

1. Use the white space on the light-house photo to add journaling.
2. Running paper through a crimper adds subtle texture.
3. Create mock photo hangers with fiber and clip rings.

Cherish

Supplies – Patterned Paper: Paperbilities; Eyelets: Creative Imaginations; Rub-on: Making Memories; Shell Charm: All The Extras; Font: Two Peas In A Bucket Blissful

Construction Tips:

1. Tape-Transfer Method:
   a. Place packing tape on top of script paper, making sure the tape is secure and there are no bubbles.
   b. Run taped paper under warm water while rubbing the back of the paper. The paper will come off and the print will remain on the tape.
   c. Quickly stick the tape onto colored paper and peel off to leave traces of color.
   d. Adhere tape to layout.
2. Braid leather strips together to create a nice accent.

Designer: Sam Cousins

Warm

Supplies – Cardstock: Paper Garden; Stickers: Karen Foster; Key: Jolee's By You; Fiber: EK Success; Tag: Making Memories; Button: Making Memories; Glue Pen: EK Success

Construction Tips:

This technique looks best with different types of fibers. Because the border is small, it is easy to use leftover scraps of fibers.

Designer: Maegan Hall

Stitching

Stitching is a creative way to accent pages. You can hand stitch with a needle and thread or use a sewing machine. Stitching can be used functionally or decoratively for embellishments, letters, borders, etc. Make stitching as understated or overstated as you wish.

Jordan - April 2004

Jordan... I love these pictures of you. On this spring morning, I wasn't even planning on taking pictures, but you were full of smiles and you were acting so funny that I thought I would give it a try. The flowers in front of the house were in full bloom and you were the perfect little model with your cowboy hat on. Once again, you filled my day with wonder, like you always do. I am so lucky to have you in my life – I love you!

Designer: Ashley Smith

You Filled My Day With Wonder

Supplies – Patterned Paper: Leisure Arts; Font: CK Hustle

Construction Tips:

Draw flower shape onto back of cardstock. Punch holes for the fibers to go through and stitch with a needle and thread.

Beauty In The Little Things

Supplies – Cardstock: DMD Designs; Vellum: DMD Designs; Thread: DMC; Label: Making Memories; Eyelets: Making Memories; Snowman Charm: Making Memories; Snowflake Charms: Mill Hill Crystal Treasures; Wire: Artistic Wire; Wire Mesh: Paragona; Glass Beads: Create-A-Craft; Fonts: St. Charles, Scrawl of the Chief, Libby Script

Construction Tips:

Draw snowflakes with pencil onto the background. Stitch clear beads to the layout with silver thread.

IT IS NO **WONDER** THAT WE SEE BEAUTY IN THE LITTLE THINGS

January 2000

secrets secrets secrets secrets

SAM AND JOSH

best friends brother best FRIENDS boys

Secrets

Supplies – Patterned Paper: Rusty Pickle; Twill Strip: 7 Gypsies; Letter Stickers: Rebecca Sower Nostalgiques; Mesh: Magic Mesh

Construction Tips:

Section your layout with zig-zag stitches.

aper Piecing

Paper piecing is a fun way to add color and design elements to your background. Piecing can also use up those scrap pieces of paper you have been collecting. Don't forget to curl, distress and tear your paper before piecing it together.

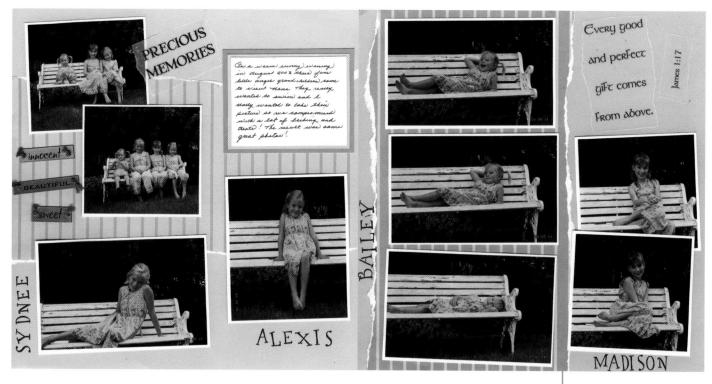

Designer: Ashley Smith

Precious Memories

Supplies — Patterned Paper: Leisure Arts;
Cardstock: DCWV; Metallic Words: DCWV

Construction Tips:
Adhere a large torn strip
of patterned paper across
a piece of cardstock.

Designer: Wanda E. Santiago

A Boy And A Box

Supplies — Patterned Paper: SEI;
Brads: Magic Scraps

Construction Tips:
1. Have photos developed with special borders to add texture without bulk.
2. Use purchased paper that gives the effect of paper piecing to save time.

Gray

Supplies — Patterned Paper:
Leisure Arts; Stickers: Leisure Arts

Construction Tips:
Combine torn pieces of vellum and patterned paper. Hide portions of the photo behind the torn vellum.

Designer: Ashley Smith

Designer: Sherrill Ghiardi Pierre

You're Perfect The Way You Are

Supplies — Patterned Paper: 7 Gypsies, Artistic
Enhancements; Cardstock: Bazzill; Letters: Making
Memories; Ribbon: Close to My Heart; Netting: Magic
Scraps; Square with Heart: Foofala; Laminate Sheet: Xyron

Construction Tips:

1. Laminate by running photo with a textured sheet of laminate through a Xyron machine.
2. Offset similar patterned paper with a solid piece of cardstock.

Godspeed Little Man

Supplies – Cardstock: WhirlWin; Vellum: Stampin' Up; Fibers: Fibers By The Yard

Construction Tips:

1. Type words from Dixie Chick's song "Godspeed" and print onto vellum for journaling.
2. Create embellishments for a layout by tear and piecing scrap pieces of paper together.

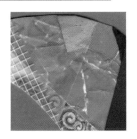

Designer: Stephanie Welsh

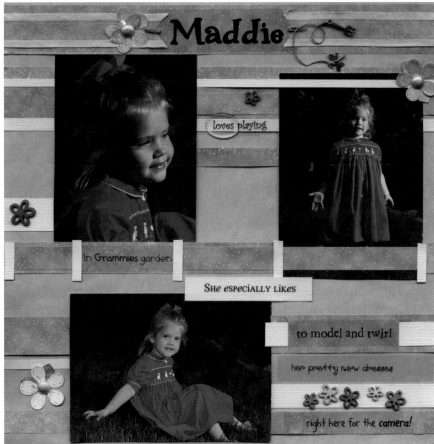

Designer: Camille Jensen

Maddie

Supplies – Patterned Paper: Leisure Arts; Cardstock: Bazzill; Conchos: Scrap Works; Punches: EK Success; Buttons: Dress It Up; Floss: Scrap Works; Metal Charms: Lost Art Treasures

Construction Tips:

Create your own patterned paper by piecing together strips of paper.

Tools

Creating a great scrapbook page can become a whole lot easier if you have the right tools and equipment. We asked some of our best designers to give us a list of the scrapbooking tools they could not live without. Here is their list:

1. Sewing Machine
2. Embossing Powder
3. Buttons
4. Wire
5. Pens/Markers
6. Scrappers' Spray
7. Stamps
8. Eyelets & Brads
9. Felt

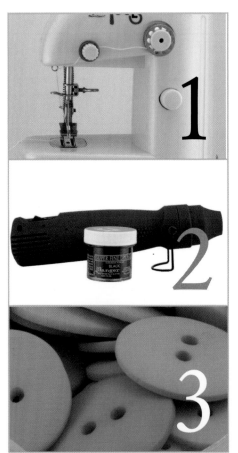